THE LIFE OF
ELIZABETH CADY STANTON

BY GILLIA M. OLSON

SEQU
ENCE

AMICUS | AMICUS INK

Sequence is published by Amicus and Amicus Ink
P.O. Box 227, Mankato, MN 56002
www.amicuspublishing.us

Library of Congress Cataloging-in-Publication Data
Names: Olson, Gillia M., author.
Title: The life of Elizabeth Cady Stanton / by Gillia M. Olson.
Description: Mankato, MN : Amicus, [2022] | Series: Sequence change maker biographies | Includes bibliographical references and index. | Audience Ages 7–10 | Audience: Grades 2–3.
Identifiers: LCCN 2019036310 (print) | LCCN 2019036311 (ebook) | ISBN 9781681519494 (library binding) | ISBN 9781681525969 (paperback) | ISBN 9781645490340 (pdf)
Subjects: LCSH: Stanton, Elizabeth Cady, 1815-1902–Juvenile literature. | Feminists–United States–Biography–Juvenile literature. | Suffragists–United States–Biography–Juvenile literature. | Women's rights–United States–History–19th century–Juvenile literature. | Women–Suffrage–United States–History–Juvenile literature.
Classification: LCC HQ1413.S67 O57 2022 (print) | LCC HQ1413.S67 (ebook) | DDC 305.42092 [B]–dc23
LC record available at https://lccn.loc.gov/2019036310
LC ebook record available at https://lccn.loc.gov/2019036311

Editor: Alissa Thielges
Designer: Ciara Beitlich
Photo Researcher: Aubrey Harper

Photo Credits: Getty/PhotoQuest cover; Wikimedia/LSE Library cover; Shutterstock/Everett Historical 4; LOC/Historic American Buildings Survey 6–7; Wikimedia/Library of Congress 8, 10–11, 12–13, 20–21; Getty/Universal History Archive 11; Alamy/Pictorial Press Ltd 12–13; Getty/Historical 15; LOC/American Press Association 16; Getty/Interim Archives 18–19; Wikimedia/University of Massachusetts, Boston 18; Wikimedia/Hartford, Conn: S.M. Betts & Company 18; Getty/Library of Congress 22–23; LOC/Samuel D. Ehrhart 24–25; Age Fotostock/Jim West 24; LOC/Carol M. Highsmith 27; Alamy/Randy Duchaine 28–29

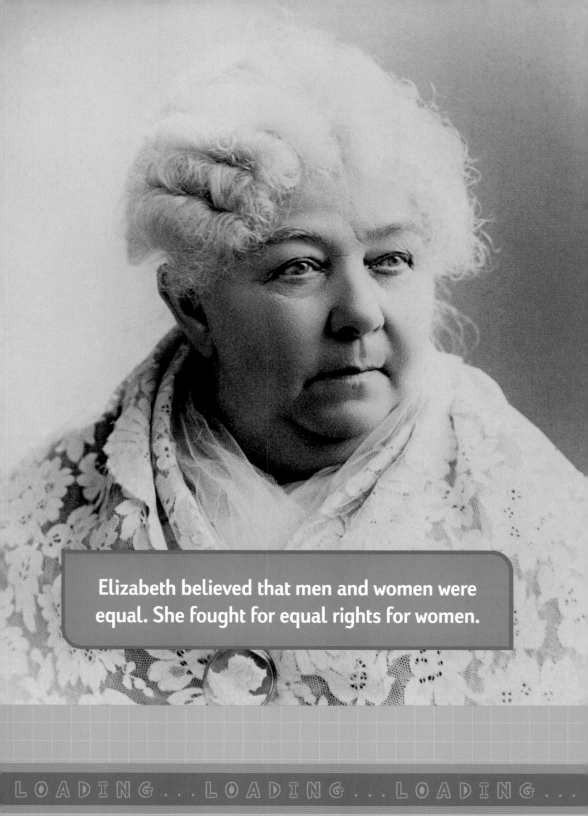

Elizabeth believed that men and women were equal. She fought for equal rights for women.

LOADING...LOADING...LOADING...

Don't Say No!

Elizabeth Cady Stanton hated being told "no." In her time, women had few **rights**. They couldn't vote. Their husbands and sons owned everything. Money that wives earned belonged to their husbands. Elizabeth was smart and confident. She knew she should have the same rights as men. She worked all her life to turn "No!" into "Yes!"

Elizabeth Cady was born November 12, 1815. Her father was a lawyer. Women came to him for help. But the law gave women few rights. Elizabeth saw how unfair it was.

When Elizabeth was 11, her brother died. She tried to comfort her father. He said, "Oh, my daughter, I wish you were a boy!" Elizabeth wanted to be all that her brother was.

Elizabeth's family lived in Johnston, New York. Later, she moved into this house in Seneca Falls.

Elizabeth is born.

NOV 12, 1815   LOADING . . . LOADING . . .

After they married, Elizabeth and Henry had children.

Elizabeth is born.

NOV 12, 1815   1840

Elizabeth marries Henry Stanton.

ING . . LOADING . . .

8

Elizabeth was very smart. In 1830, she graduated high school. She wanted to go to Union College. But only boys could go there. She went to a girl's **seminary** school instead.

She met Henry Stanton in 1839. Henry gave speeches about ending **slavery**. In 1840, Elizabeth and Henry got married. She had "promise to obey" taken out of their wedding **vows**.

Women's Rights and Ending Slavery

The Stantons moved to Seneca Falls, New York, in 1847. They had seven children. Elizabeth loved raising her children. But she wanted other work, too. Elizabeth and other women held a women's rights **convention**. More than 300 people came. Elizabeth helped write out their goals. They included voting rights for women, called **suffrage**.

Elizabeth is born.

Elizabeth helps organize the first women's rights convention.

NOV 12, 1815   1840   1848   . . L O A D I N G . . .

Elizabeth marries Henry Stanton.

THE FIRST CONVENTION

EVER CALLED TO DISCUSS THE

Civil and Political Rights of Women,

SENECA FALLS, N. Y., JULY 19, 20, 1848.

———

WOMAN'S RIGHTS CONVENTION.

———

A Convention to discuss the social, civil, and religious condition and rights of woman will be held in the Wesleyan Chapel, at Seneca Falls, N. Y., on Wednesday and Thursday, the 19th and 20th of July current; commencing at 10 o'clock A. M. During the first day the meeting will be exclusively for women, who are earnestly invited to attend. The public generally are invited to be present on the second day, when Lucretia Mott, of Philadelphia, and other ladies and gentlemen, will address the Convention.*

———

* This call was published in the *Seneca County Courier*, July 14, 1848, without any signatures. The movers of this Convention, who drafted the call, the declaration and resolutions were Elizabeth Cady Stanton, Lucretia Mott, Martha C. Wright, Mary Ann McClintock, and Jane C. Hunt.

Elizabeth helped write a message to tell people about the convention.

LOADING... LOADING... LOADING...

Elizabeth is born.

Elizabeth helps organize the first women's rights convention.

NOV 12, 1815   1840   1848   1851   ADING . . .

Elizabeth marries Henry Stanton.

Elizabeth meets Susan B. Anthony.

Elizabeth met Susan B. Anthony in 1851. They would go on to have a 50-year friendship. They both worked for women's rights and to end slavery. Elizabeth was a great writer. Susan was a great organizer. They made an excellent team. Elizabeth would often write speeches. Susan would travel around the country and give them.

Lifelong friends Elizabeth and Susan (right) worked hard for women's rights.

LOADING . . . LOADING . . . LOADING . . .

Slavery ended during the **U.S. Civil War**. Shortly after, the 14th **Amendment** was proposed. It said all former slaves were U.S. citizens. As citizens, African Americans could vote. But women could not vote. Elizabeth tried to get voting rights for all women included. It didn't work. Many people thought women could wait. The 14th Amendment passed in 1868.

An African American man votes for mayor as white men scowl at him.

Elizabeth is born.

Elizabeth helps organize the first women's rights convention.

Elizabeth tries to get the 14th Amendment to include women.

NOV 12, 1815   1840   1848   1851   1866

Elizabeth marries Henry Stanton.

Elizabeth meets Susan B. Anthony.

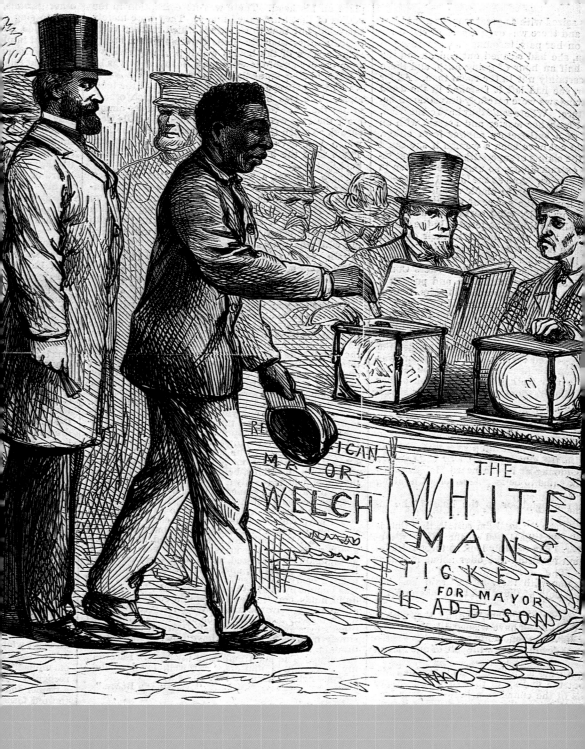

Women walk in a parade in 1912 in support of women's suffrage.

Elizabeth is born.

Elizabeth helps organize the first women's rights convention.

Elizabeth tries to get the 14th Amendment to include women.

NOV 12, 1815   1840   1848   1851   1866   1869

Elizabeth marries Henry Stanton.

Elizabeth meets Susan B. Anthony.

Elizabeth and Susan start the NWSA.

Rebel with a Cause

Elizabeth wanted to help women beyond voting rights. Women needed better work opportunities. Divorce laws were unfair. Elizabeth and Susan started the National Women Suffrage Association (NWSA). It worked for voting rights and these other issues. Another group, the American Woman Suffrage Association (AWSA), focused only on suffrage.

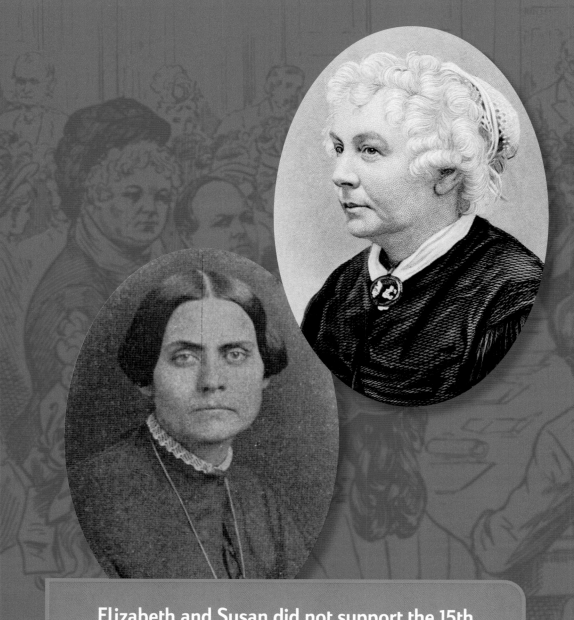

Elizabeth and Susan did not support the 15th Amendment. They wanted women's suffrage, too.

Elizabeth is born.

Elizabeth helps organize the first women's rights convention.

Elizabeth tries to get the 14th Amendment to include women.

NOV 12, 1815   1840   1848   1851   1866   1869

Elizabeth marries Henry Stanton.

Elizabeth meets Susan B. Anthony.

Elizabeth and Susan start the NWSA.

Elizabeth and Susan worked state-by-state for women's rights. In 1869, Elizabeth signed up for a speech tour. She and Susan traveled the country. Elizabeth was a great speaker.

Some people thought the 14th Amendment didn't give black men voting rights. In 1870, the 15th Amendment passed. It said men of any race can vote. But women were left out again.

15th Amendment passes; black men can vote, but women still can't.

1870

L O A D I N G . . . L O A D I N G . . .

Did the 14th and 15th amendments allow women to vote? Some women thought so. They tried to vote. Some were arrested. The others were blocked. Elizabeth tried in 1880, but she was blocked.

Susan and Elizabeth kept pushing for new laws. They got a senator to introduce a new amendment. It would give women the right to vote. But Congress would not pass it.

Women vote illegally in a New York election in 1917.

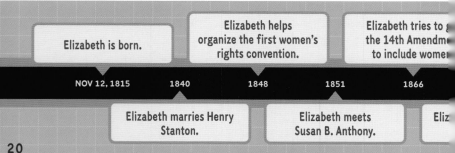

Elizabeth is born.		Elizabeth helps organize the first women's rights convention.		Elizabeth tries to g the 14th Amendm to include women
NOV 12, 1815	1840	1848	1851	1866
	Elizabeth marries Henry Stanton.		Elizabeth meets Susan B. Anthony.	Eliz

15th Amendment passes; black men can vote, but women still can't.

1870   1880

LOADING... LOADING...

Elizabeth attempts to vote in an election and is denied.

Elizabeth sits with other founding members of the International Council of Women.

Elizabeth is born.

Elizabeth helps organize the first women's rights convention.

Elizabeth tries to get the 14th Amendment to include women.

NOV 12, 1815   1840   1848   1851   1866   1869

Elizabeth marries Henry Stanton.

Elizabeth meets Susan B. Anthony.

Elizabeth and Susan start the NWSA.

Writing History

Elizabeth had big ideas. Between 1881 and 1886, she, Susan, and Matilda Joslyn Gage wrote *History of Woman Suffrage*. She also took action. In 1888, the NWSA founded the International Council of Women (ICW). It works for women's rights all over the world.

In 1890, the NWSA and AWSA became the National American Woman Suffrage Association (NAWSA). Elizabeth was elected its president.

15th Amendment passes; black men can vote, but women still can't.

Elizabeth is elected president of NAWSA.

1870 1880 1890 3 . . . LOADING . . .

Elizabeth attempts to vote in an election and is denied.

Over the years, Elizabeth questioned **Christianity**. She thought the religion didn't show women as equal to men. In 1895 and 1898, she published *The Woman's Bible*. In it, she said religion was one reason for women's lack of rights. It was very shocking for the time. The NAWSA worried her ideas would hurt their work. They did not support the book.

THE WOMAN'S BIBLE

ELIZABETH CADY STANTON

A political cartoon shows a man stopping a woman from speaking about women's rights.

Elizabeth is born.

Elizabeth helps organize the first women's rights convention.

Elizabeth tries to get the 14th Amendment to include women.

NOV 12, 1815   1840   1848   1851   1866   1869

Elizabeth marries Henry Stanton.

Elizabeth meets Susan B. Anthony.

Elizabeth and Susan start the NWSA.

"Don't pay any attention to this woman-suffrage talk. *Your* place is in the home, caring for the children."

15th Amendment passes; black men can vote, but women still can't.

Elizabeth is elected president of NAWSA.

1870   1880   1890   1895

Elizabeth attempts to vote in an election and is denied.

First volume of *The Woman's Bible* is published.

A Woman's Work

As Elizabeth got older, she wanted to write down her life story. She wrote *Eighty Years and More*. It was about her childhood and early life. She continued to write until her death in 1902.

Though Elizabeth couldn't go to college, both her daughters did. They went to Vassar College. Both went on to earn graduate degrees.

Elizabeth is born.

Elizabeth helps organize the first women's rights convention.

Elizabeth tries to get the 14th Amendment to include women.

NOV 12, 1815   1840   1848   1851   1866   1869

Elizabeth marries Henry Stanton.

Elizabeth meets Susan B. Anthony.

Elizabeth and Susan start the NWSA.

For 50 years, Elizabeth used her writing to push for women's rights.

15th Amendment passes; black men can vote, but women still can't.

Elizabeth is elected president of NAWSA.

Elizabeth dies at age 86.

1870   1880   1890   1895   OCT 26, 1902   N G . . .

Elizabeth attempts to vote in an election and is denied.

First volume of *The Woman's Bible* is published.

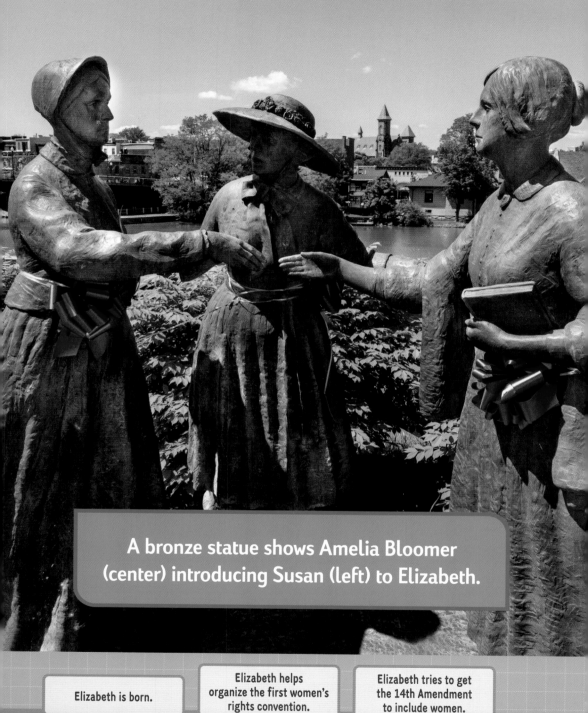

A bronze statue shows Amelia Bloomer (center) introducing Susan (left) to Elizabeth.

Elizabeth is born.

Elizabeth helps organize the first women's rights convention.

Elizabeth tries to get the 14th Amendment to include women.

NOV 12, 1815   1840   1848   1851   1866   1869

Elizabeth marries Henry Stanton.

Elizabeth meets Susan B. Anthony.

Elizabeth and Susan start the NWSA.

Elizabeth didn't live to see women get to vote in 1920. But her work made it possible. In 1998, New York marked the 150th anniversary of the Seneca Falls convention. They built a statue. It is called *When Anthony Met Stanton*. It honors Elizabeth and Susan as leaders of women's rights. Their hard work lets us celebrate 100 years and more of women's suffrage.

15th Amendment passes; black men can vote, but women still can't.

Elizabeth is elected president of NAWSA.

Elizabeth dies at age 86.

1870   1880   1890   1895   OCT 26, 1902   2020

Elizabeth attempts to vote in an election and is denied.

First volume of *The Woman's Bible* is published.

The 100th anniversary of women's right to vote.

Glossary

amendment A law that is added to the United States Constitution, voted on by Congress, and agreed to by the states.

Christianity A religion based on the belief of Jesus and his teachings.

convention A formal meeting to talk and act on things that concern a particular group.

right Something a person is legally entitled to do.

seminary A school for post-secondary education that has some similarities to a college but does not give bachelor's degrees.

slavery When people are owned by another person, forced to work, and can be sold at the owner's will.

suffrage The right to vote.

U.S. Civil War A war from 1861 to 1865 between the northern and southern states of the United States over the enslavement of African Americans.

vow A serious and important promise.

Read More

Gillibrand, Kirsten. *Bold & Brave: Ten Heroes Who Won Women the Right to Vote.* New York: Random House Children's Books, 2018.

Jenner, Caryn. *Winning the Vote for Women.* New York: Kingfisher, 2019.

Stoltman, Joan. *Elizabeth Cady Stanton.* New York: Gareth Stevens Publishing, 2019.

Websites

America's Story | Elizabeth Cady Stanton
http://www.americaslibrary.gov/aa/stanton/aa_stanton_subj.html

NWHM | Timeline: Woman Suffrage
https://www.womenshistory.org/exhibits/timeline-woman-suffrage

PBS | A Great Partnership
https://www.pbs.org/video/great-partnership-rdabec/

Index

About the Author

Gillia M. Olson is a former farm girl turned writer. She's written and
edited children's books for more than 20 years. She hopes stories of
great women will inspire her daughter someday, just as they have
inspired her. She lives in southern Minnesota.